BOBBY LAYNE, BARRY SANDERS, CORY SCHLESINGER, HERMAN MOORE, GAIL COGDILL, CHARLIE SANDERS, LOU CREEKMUR, LOMAS BROWN, HARLEY SEWELL, JOHN GORDY, ED FLANAGAN, AL BAKER, ROBERT PORCHER, ALEX KARRAS, DOUG ENGLISH, JOE SCHMIDT, WAYNE WALKER, CHRIS SPIELMAN, LEM BARNEY, DICK "NIGHT TRAIN" LANE, DICK LEBEAU, JACK CHRISTIANSEN, JASON HANSON, YALE LARY, BOBBY LAYNE, BARRY SANDERS, CORY SCHLESINGER, HERMAN MOORE, GAIL COGDILL, CHARLIE SANDERS, LOU CREEKMUR, LOMAS BROWN, HARLEY

THE STORY OF THE DETROIT LIONS

THE STORY OF THE
DETROIT LIONS

BY JIM WHITING

CREATIVE EDUCATION / CREATIVE PAPERBACKS

PUBLISHED BY CREATIVE EDUCATION AND CREATIVE PAPERBACKS
P.O. BOX 227, MANKATO, MINNESOTA 56002
CREATIVE EDUCATION AND CREATIVE PAPERBACKS ARE IMPRINTS OF THE
CREATIVE COMPANY
WWW.THECREATIVECOMPANY.US

DESIGN AND PRODUCTION BY BLUE DESIGN (WWW.BLUEDES.COM)
ART DIRECTION BY RITA MARSHALL
PRINTED IN CHINA

PHOTOGRAPHS BY AP IMAGES (AP, ASSOCIATED PRESS), GETTY IMAGES
(BETTMANN, VERNON BIEVER, CLIFTON BOUTELLE/NFL PHOTOS,
SCOTT CUNNINGHAM, TOM DAHLIN, DIAMOND IMAGES, FOCUS ON SPORT,
GEORGE GELATLY/NFL, WALTER IOOSS JR./SI, NEIL LEIFER/SI, JORGE LEMUS/
NURPHOTO, RONALD MARTINEZ, CHRIS MCGRATH, NFL, DARRYL NORENBERG/
NFL, PRO FOOTBALL HALL OF FAME, MICHAEL REAVES/STRINGER, ROBERT
RIGER, JOE ROBBINS, BILL SMITH)

NAMES: WHITING, JIM, AUTHOR.
TITLE: THE STORY OF THE DETROIT LIONS / JIM WHITING.
SERIES: NFL TODAY.
INCLUDES INDEX.
SUMMARY: THIS HIGH-INTEREST HISTORY OF THE NATIONAL FOOTBALL
LEAGUE'S DETROIT LIONS HIGHLIGHTS MEMORABLE GAMES, SUMMARIZES
SEASONAL TRIUMPHS AND DEFEATS, AND FEATURES STANDOUT PLAYERS SUCH
AS MATTHEW STAFFORD.
IDENTIFIERS: LCCN 2018059634 / ISBN 978-1-64026-140-2 (HARDCOVER) / ISBN
978-1-62832-703-8 (PBK) / ISBN 978-1-64000-258-6 (EBOOK)
SUBJECTS: LCSH: DETROIT LIONS (FOOTBALL TEAM)—HISTORY—JUVENILE
LITERATURE.
CLASSIFICATION: LCC GV956.D4 W47 2019 / DDC 796.332/640977434—DC23

FIRST EDITION HC 9 8 7 6 5 4 3 2 1
FIRST EDITION PBK 9 8 7 6 5 4 3 2 1

COVER: MATTHEW STAFFORD
PAGE 2: KERRYON JOHNSON
PAGES 6–7: ERNIE SIMS

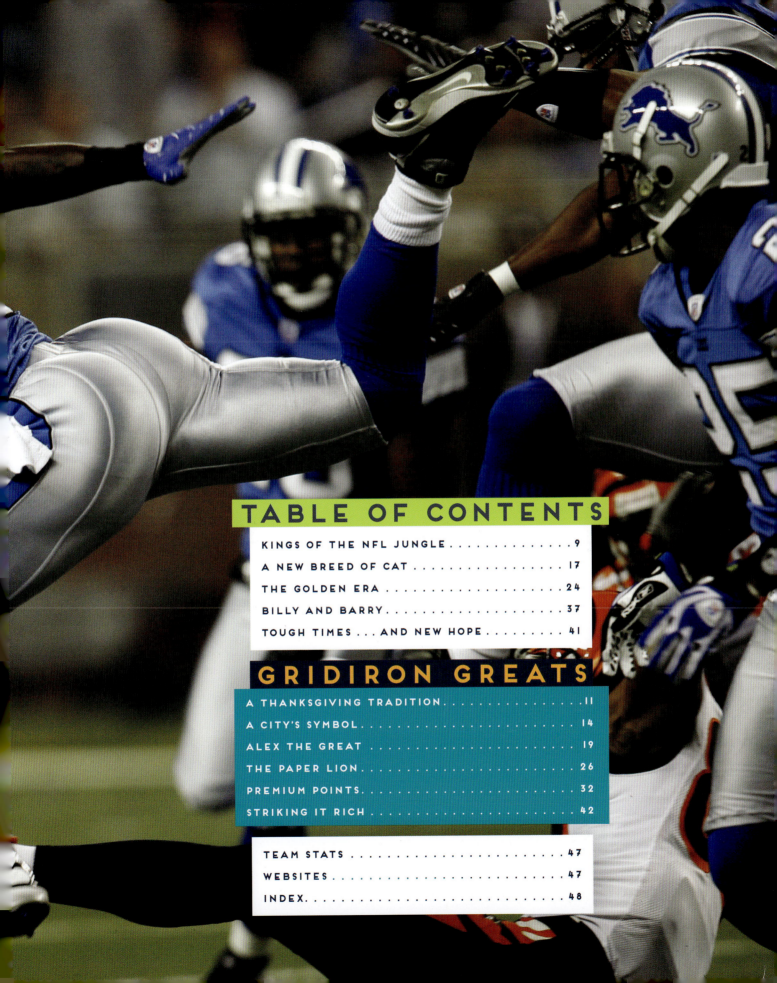

TABLE OF CONTENTS

GRIDIRON GREATS

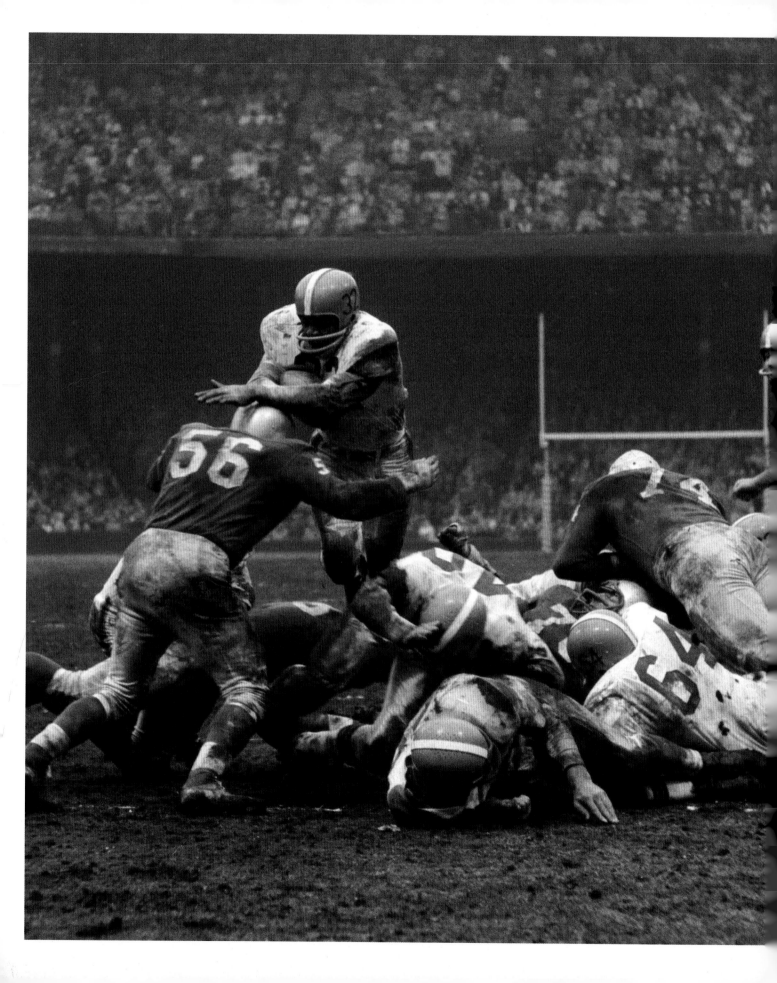

KINGS OF THE NFL JUNGLE

During much of the 1950s, the two best teams in the National Football League (NFL) were the Cleveland Browns and the Detroit Lions. They met for the league championship in 1952, 1953, and 1954. The Lions won the first two matchups. Then Cleveland thrashed them, 56–10, in the third. On December 29, 1957, the two teams were at it again. The Browns were slight favorites. They featured Rookie of the Year Jim Brown. He had rushed for nearly 1,000 yards during the season. Earlier in the month, Lions quarterback Bobby Layne had suffered a broken leg. His replacement was Tobin Rote. Rote had been a quarterback with the Green Bay Packers for seven years. He had joined Detroit at the start of the season.

DETROIT LIONS

Detroit was fortunate to be playing for the title. It had finished the season with an 8–4 record. This left it tied with the San Francisco 49ers for the West Division's best record. Each team had won one of their two regular-season games. So the league ordered a playoff. It was held at San Francisco's Kezar Stadium. The 49ers had home-field advantage. They took a 27–7 lead early in the third quarter. But Rote led a furious comeback. The Lions roared to a 28–27 lead in the fourth quarter. Jim Martin tacked on a field goal to seal the win. The game is remembered as one of the NFL's greatest comebacks.

The extra game meant the Lions had only one week to get ready for the title game. Cleveland had an extra week

LEFT: EARLY 1950S LIONS

GRIDIRON GREATS
A THANKSGIVING TRADITION

In their first NFL season, the Lions drew small crowds. Owner George Richards wanted to attract more fans. He decided to play a game on Thanksgiving Day. He convinced NBC to broadcast it on nationwide radio. The Lions faced the undefeated Chicago Bears. They were the team's closest and fiercest rivals. A crowd of 25,000 packed the stadium. Several thousand fans were turned away. Since then, the Thanksgiving game has been celebrated in Detroit nearly every year. Two other games have been added on Thanksgiving as well. This gives football fans plenty of pigskin to go with their turkey.

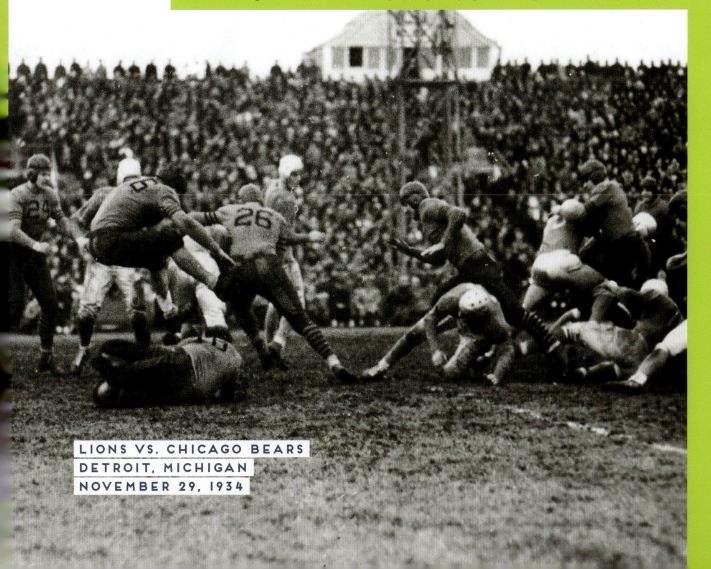

LIONS VS. CHICAGO BEARS
DETROIT, MICHIGAN
NOVEMBER 29, 1934

END STEVE JUNKER

"ALL THE TENSION BUILT UP BEFORE LAST SUNDAY'S WESTERN DIVISION PLAYOFF AGAINST SAN FRANCISCO WAS GONE."

—COACH GEORGE WILSON

to rest and prepare. Once the game started, though, the Browns were the ones who looked tired. Rote led Detroit to a 17–0 first quarter lead. Brown had a 29-yard touchdown run in the second quarter. It gave Cleveland fans a glimmer of hope. But that hope soon vanished. Detroit scored two more touchdowns before halftime. The Lions went on to demolish the Browns, 59–14. Rote finished with 280 passing yards. He threw four touchdowns and ran for another. "All the tension built up before last Sunday's Western Division playoff against San Francisco was gone," said Detroit coach George Wilson. "We just couldn't be anything but relaxed against the Browns."

DETROIT LIONS

13

GRIDIRON GREATS v
A CITY'S SYMBOL

Bobby Layne joined the Detroit Lions in 1950 by way of a trade with the New York Bulldogs. He was known for late-night partying and underachievement. But Lions fans came to love the free-spirited quarterback. "He was the symbol of this city, the toughest and best," said Detroit sports columnist Jerry Green. Layne's final full season with the Lions was 1957. It was bittersweet. He helped the team get to the NFL Championship Game. But he couldn't play in it. He had broken a leg. The Lions traded Layne to the Pittsburgh Steelers early in the 1958 season.

196

196 CAREER PASSING TOUCHDOWNS

243

243 CAREER INTERCEPTIONS

A NEW BREED OF CAT

n the early 1930s, the United States was mired in the Great Depression. Even in a working-class city such as Detroit, good jobs were hard to find. Life in the "Motor City" had few luxuries. One exception was the Detroit Tigers baseball team. When it won the American League championship in 1934, the city cheered. Radio tycoon and sports enthusiast George Richards took note. He bought the financially struggling Portsmouth Spartans. Then he

28 YARDS (LONGEST INTERCEPTION RETURN)

161 GAMES PLAYED

ALEX KARRAS
DEFENSIVE TACKLE

LIONS SEASONS: 1958-62, 1964-70
HEIGHT: 6-FOOT-2
WEIGHT: 248 POUNDS

GRIDIRON GREATS v
ALEX THE GREAT

Alex Karras frightened opponents. The "Mad Duck" was capable of singlehandedly collapsing offensive lines. He was fast and relentless in his pursuit. Offensive linemen could not match his speed. Sometimes running backs couldn't, either. "Running away from Karras is worse than running at him," said Baltimore Colts running back Lenny Moore. "He moves so fast on those stumpy legs, and you can hear him closing in on you from behind. I hate that sound. You get this feeling like you're about to be buried by a buffalo stampede." Karras also wrestled professionally. He went on to act in movies such as *Blazing Saddles*.

moved them from Ohio to Detroit. Keeping the city's big cat theme, Richards renamed his team the Lions. "The lion is the monarch of the jungle, and we hope to be the monarch of the league," he said.

The team roared out of the gate. It won its first 10 games. Seven were shutouts. Detroit's first loss came during its inaugural Thanksgiving Day game. This tradition continues today. But in 1934, it meant the Lions played three games in just eight days. They lost all three by three points each. They barely missed the playoffs.

In 1935, Detroit leaped all the way to the NFL Championship Game. Freezing rain turned the field into a muddy mess. But the Lions mauled the New York Giants, 26–7. They were league champions! One of the stars was tailback Dutch Clark. He was the first great Lions rusher. He was famous for his cool leadership. "If Dutch stepped on the field with [football legends] Red Grange, Jim

"IF DUTCH STEPPED ON THE FIELD WITH [FOOTBALL LEGENDS] RED GRANGE, JIM THORPE, AND GEORGE GIPP, DUTCH WOULD BE THE GENERAL."

—AN OPPOSING COACH

Thorpe, and George Gipp," an opposing coach said, "Dutch would be the general."

The Lions compiled winning records for the rest of the 1930s. They didn't win any more titles, though. In the 1940s, Detroit had some of the NFL's brightest stars. Alex Wojciechowicz was an undersized center and linebacker. He was a fierce player. Bill Dudley was a versatile running back and kick returner. His nickname was "Bullet Bill." But this decade was difficult for the team. In 1942, the Lions did not win a single game. They finished with winning records just twice, in 1944 and 1945.

BILL DUDLEY

THE GOLDEN ERA

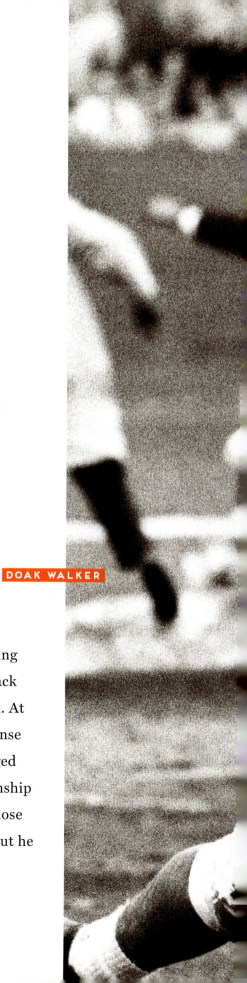

Things finally began looking up in 1950. That year, Detroit acquired Bobby Layne. It added halfback Doak Walker, too. Hulking lineman Leon Hart also boosted the team. At 6-foot-5 and 257 pounds, he was a huge athlete who played both offense and defense. The Lions finished with a 6–6 mark. In 1951, they charged to 7–4–1. Suddenly, Detroit was back. It played in the NFL Championship Game in four of the next six years. The player most responsible for those good times was Layne. His career statistics were not extraordinary. But he

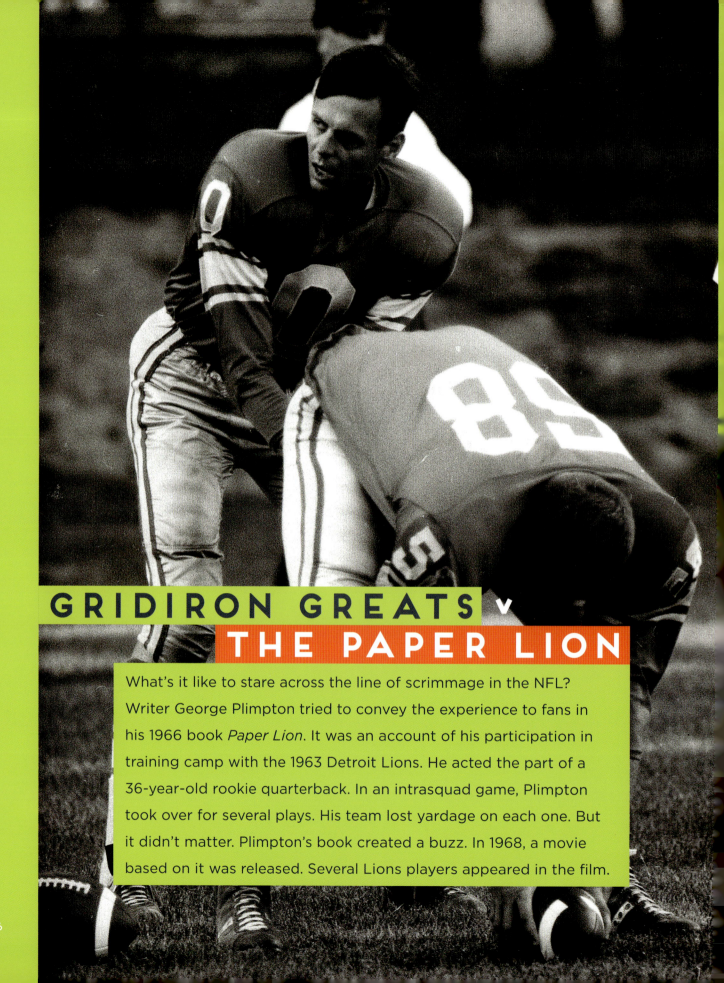

GRIDIRON GREATS v

THE PAPER LION

What's it like to stare across the line of scrimmage in the NFL? Writer George Plimpton tried to convey the experience to fans in his 1966 book *Paper Lion*. It was an account of his participation in training camp with the 1963 Detroit Lions. He acted the part of a 36-year-old rookie quarterback. In an intrasquad game, Plimpton took over for several plays. His team lost yardage on each one. But it didn't matter. Plimpton's book created a buzz. In 1968, a movie based on it was released. Several Lions players appeared in the film.

24

24 PASSING TOUCHDOWNS FOR EARL MORRALL IN 1963

13

13 RECEIVING TOUCHDOWNS FOR TERRY BARR IN 1963

was a natural leader. Layne's toughness was unmatched. He could be fiery when the situation called for it. But he preferred to inspire his teammates with his calm attitude. He often cracked jokes in the huddle during tense moments. Layne hated defeat. He refused to believe his team could be beaten. "Bobby never lost a game," Walker once said. "The clock just ran out on him a couple of times, that's all."

In 1952, the Lions went 9–3. They defeated Cleveland for the NFL championship. The 1953 title game fueled Layne's legend. The game was down to the last four minutes. Cleveland led, 16–10. The Lions went to their huddle. Layne saw nervousness in his teammates' eyes. "Y'all block," he said in his whisky voice, "and ol' Bobby'll pass you right to the championship." Eight plays later, he threw a 33-yard touchdown pass to Jim Doran. (A defensive end, Doran had taken Hart's place when the receiver was injured earlier in the game.) The score was

now tied. Walker booted home the extra point to put Detroit ahead. The Lions were league champs for the second year in a row. Three years later, they added another NFL title. But early in 1958, Detroit fans said goodbye to their great leader. Layne was traded away.

Without Layne, the Lions took a step back. They finished second in their division in 1960, 1961, and 1962. Still, they had a fierce defense.

SAFETY YALE LARY

GRIDIRON GREATS V
PREMIUM POINTS

In 1970, a strong offensive attack carried the Lions into the playoffs. They went up against the Dallas Cowboys. Defense was the name of the game. Dallas kicked a field goal in the first quarter. It added a safety in the fourth. The Lions were scoreless. In the last minute of play, they drove to the Cowboy's 29-yard line. They hoped for a game-winning touchdown. But Dallas intercepted a pass by Lions quarterback Bill Munson. Dallas won, 5–0. It was the lowest-scoring playoff game in NFL history. Only two other NFL games have ended with the same final score.

76 LIONS TOTAL RUSHING YARDS

80 LIONS PASSING YARDS

Joe Schmidt was an aggressive linebacker. He mastered the "red dog" blitz play. Safety Yale Lary was one of the game's top ballhawks. He nabbed 50 interceptions during his Lions career. Cornerback Dick "Night Train" Lane earned a fearsome reputation as a headhunter. He often hit opposing ball carriers high and hard.

The Detroit defense proved just how good it was in 1962. The Lions played a classic Thanksgiving Day game against the undefeated Packers. The Lions swarmed the Packers' great quarterback, Bart Starr. They sacked him 10 times. By the start of the fourth quarter, Detroit led 26–0. It went on to win 26–14. One sportswriter called it "one of the most memorable displays of aggressive defensive football ever witnessed." But the Lions' defense was not good enough to bring home another NFL title. The team finished the year at 11–3. After that, victories were hard to come by.

BILLY AND BARRY

As the 1970s began, the Lions were eager to return to championship form. But the decade proved to be largely frustrating. The Minnesota Vikings ruled the new National Football Conference (NFC) Central Division. Detroit usually finished behind Minnesota.

In 1979, the Lions stumbled. They won just two games. The poor record gave them the first pick in the 1980 NFL Draft. The team selected speedy running back Billy Sims. He had won the Heisman Trophy in 1978 as the nation's best college football player. The Lions hoped Sims would provide the boost they so badly needed. He did. Sims set a team record by piling up 1,303 rushing yards. He scored 16 touchdowns, too. Sims was named Rookie of the Year. The Lions finished the season at 9–7. "I must admit," said head coach Monte Clark, "as much as I like to stress team effort, Billy has been the big difference."

Detroit continued to improve. It made the postseason in 1982 and 1983. The Washington Redskins knocked the team out in the 1982 Wild Card. The Lions faced the 49ers in the 1983 playoffs. Sims scored two fourth-quarter touchdowns to put the Lions up 23–17. Five minutes remained. San Francisco quarterback Joe Montana led his team to a late touchdown. The 49ers took the lead, 24–23. Lions kicker Eddie Murray attempted a 43-yard field goal with five seconds left. He missed by inches. The next season was a disaster. The Lions won just four games. In Week 8, Sims suffered a severe knee injury. He never played another game. When Sims went down, the Lions went down with him.

The 1989 season felt a bit like 1980 all over again. The Lions had won just four games in each of the two previous seasons. They received the third pick in the 1989 Draft. Again, they chose a star running back. This one was Barry Sanders. He quickly proved to be even better than Sims. Sanders was named Rookie of the Year. He finished the season with 1,470 rushing yards. That broke Sims's team record.

Sanders was just getting started. He would go on to enjoy one of the most amazing careers in NFL history. In his 10 years with the team, he rushed for 15,269 yards. That was an average of nearly 1,527 yards per year! And he did it in electrifying style. He combined great balance with vision and strength. He could move like no other runner. "Barry is so good that sometimes during a game, I catch myself watching as a fan and not an opponent," said opposing linebacker Hardy Nickerson. "He does things that leave even pros' mouths hanging open."

Behind Sanders, the team clawed its way to 12 wins in 1991. It was Detroit's best-ever mark. The Lions faced the Dallas Cowboys in the playoffs. They crushed the Cowboys, 38–6. It was their first playoff victory since 1957. However, the Redskins dashed their championship hopes. Washington trounced Detroit, 41–10, in the NFC Championship Game.

From 1993 to 1997, the Lions qualified for the playoffs four times. Each time, they lost in the Wild Card. Sanders charged for 2,053 rushing yards in 1997. He was only the third running back to top the prestigious 2,000-yard mark. After the 1998 season, Sanders announced his retirement. The Lions reeled. The announcement stunned the sports world. Sanders was just 30 years old. If he had kept playing, he likely would have topped Walter Payton's record for career rushing yards. But the humble star felt the timing was right. "I always told myself I would play this game as long as it was fun," he explained. "When it became a job for me, I decided it was time to move on."

BARRY SANDERS

TOUGH TIMES ...
AND NEW HOPE

Suddenly, the Lions roster had a gaping hole. Even without Sanders, Detroit squeezed into the playoffs in 1999. Two years later, the Lions hit a low point. They lost 14 games. They gave up more points than any other team in the NFC. Detroit lost 13 games the following year. It remained the worst defense in the conference. More losing seasons followed. In 2007, hopes were rekindled. Veteran quarterback Jon Kitna provided a driving force. Detroit had not seen a quarterback with his passion and leadership for many years. The Lions rolled to a 6–2 start. But then the team imploded. It lost seven of its final eight games. The losing slide carried into the following season. Three different quarterbacks played equally poorly for the Lions. The running game was mediocre. The

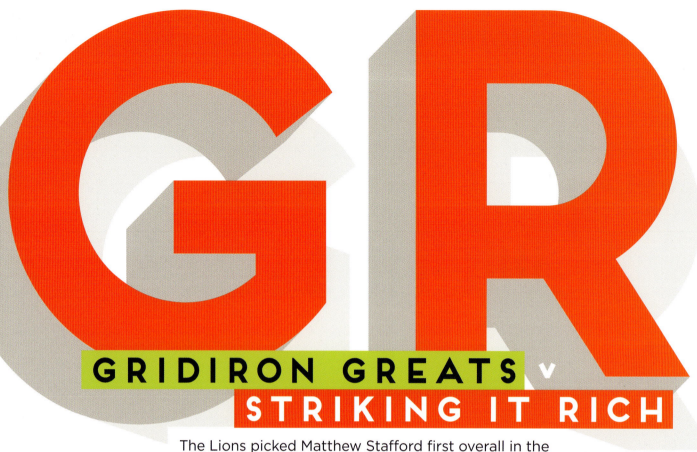

GRIDIRON GREATS v
STRIKING IT RICH

The Lions picked Matthew Stafford first overall in the 2009 Draft. He became Detroit's starting quarterback to open the 2009 season. He was an instant hit. He became the youngest player to throw five touchdown passes in a game. He has continued at that high level. In 2011, he became just the fourth quarterback to surpass 5,000 passing yards in a season. Five years later, he set an NFL record. He led Detroit to eight comeback wins in a season. In 2017, he received a $135 million contract extension. For a time, this made him the highest-paid player in NFL history.

MATTHEW STAFFORD
QUARTERBACK

LIONS SEASONS: 2009-PRESENT
HEIGHT: 6-FOOT-3
WEIGHT: 220 POUNDS

DETROIT LIONS

43

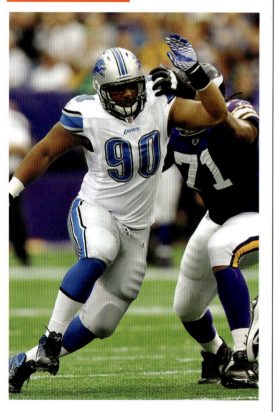

NDAMUKONG SUH

defense struggled. The 2008 Lions were the first team in NFL history to lose all 16 of its games.

The Lions had the top overall pick in the 2009 Draft. With it, they nabbed Matthew Stafford. He was a strong-armed quarterback from the University of Georgia. Three games into the year, they won. The cycle of losing was broken! Unfortunately, they managed only one more win during the season. In the 2010 Draft, Detroit picked second. It chose Ndamukong Suh. He was a powerful defensive tackle with a mean streak. Stafford was sidelined for most of the season by a shoulder injury. Still, the Lions improved to 6–10.

In 2011, Stafford was back at the helm. Detroit rattled off five straight wins. The Lions finished the season with 10 wins. They earned their first playoff berth in 12 years. One reason was wide receiver Calvin "Megatron" Johnson. At 6-foot-5 and 237 pounds, he was big and fast. The Lions met the New Orleans Saints in the playoffs. The game proved to be a high-scoring affair. Stafford threw for 3 touchdowns and 380 yards. Still, the Lions came up short. They were disappointed. But they believed they had just begun to hit their stride. "It's a learning experience for the whole team," said coach Jim Schwartz. "We'll get better. We'll be back."

Schwartz was right. The Lions returned to the playoffs in 2014. They faced Dallas in the Wild Card. The Lions pounced to an early 14-point lead. But they couldn't hold it. The Cowboys caught up and won, 24–20. Two years

CALVIN JOHNSON

LINEBACKER JARRAD DAVIS

later, Detroit was back in the playoffs. Unfortunately, the Seattle Seahawks cruised to an easy win. Despite posting back-to-back winning seasons for the first time since 1995, the Lions missed the playoffs in 2017. They dropped back to a 6–10 finish the following year.

The Detroit Lions got their start during the Great Depression. They were a welcome distraction for hard-pressed Motor City workers. But after capturing their fourth NFL title, the Lions entered a slump of their own. They won just a single playoff game in a span lasting more than 60 years. Today, fans can't wait for the Lions to be kings of the gridiron again.

NFL CHAMPIONSHIPS

1935, 1952, 1953, 1957

WEBSITES

DETROIT LIONS
https://www.detroitlions.com/

NFL: DETROIT LIONS TEAM PAGE
http://www.nfl.com/teams/detroitlions/profile?team=DET

DETROIT LIONS

INDEX

WIDE RECEIVER HERMAN MOORE